COUNTRIES OF THE WORLD

Iraq

by Rebecca Sabelko

BELLWETHER MEDIA • MINNEAPOLIS, MN

Blastoff! Readers are carefully developed by literacy experts to build reading stamina and move students toward fluency by combining standards-based content with developmentally appropriate text.

Level 1 provides the most support through repetition of high-frequency words, light text, predictable sentence patterns, and strong visual support.

Level 2 offers early readers a bit more challenge through varied sentences, increased text load, and text-supportive special features.

Level 3 advances early-fluent readers toward fluency through increased text load, less reliance on photos, advancing concepts, longer sentences, and more complex special features.

★ **Blastoff! Universe**

Reading Level

Grade
K

Grades
1–3

Grade
4

This edition first published in 2023 by Bellwether Media, Inc.

No part of this publication may be reproduced in whole or in part without written permission of the publisher. For information regarding permission, write to Bellwether Media, Inc., Attention: Permissions Department, 6012 Blue Circle Drive, Minnetonka, MN 55343.

Library of Congress Cataloging-in-Publication Data

Names: Sabelko, Rebecca, author.
Title: Iraq / by Rebecca Sabelko.
Description: Minneapolis, MN : Bellwether Media, 2023. | Series: Blastoff! readers : countries of the world | Includes bibliographical references and index. | Audience: Ages 5-8 | Audience: Grades 2-3 | Summary: "Relevant images match informative text in this introduction to Iraq. Intended for students in kindergarten through third grade"–Provided by publisher.
Identifiers: LCCN 2022018244 (print) | LCCN 2022018245 (ebook) | ISBN 9781644877203 (library binding) | ISBN 9781648347665 (ebook)
Subjects: LCSH: Iraq–Juvenile literature.
Classification: LCC DS70.62 .S23 2023 (print) | LCC DS70.62 (ebook) | DDC 56.7–dc23/eng/20220429
LC record available at https://lccn.loc.gov/2022018244
LC ebook record available at https://lccn.loc.gov/2022018245

Editor: Rachael Barnes   Designer: Gabriel Hilger

Printed in the United States of America, North Mankato, MN.

Table of Contents

All About Iraq

Baghdad

Iraq is a country in the **Middle East**. This area is in southwestern Asia. The capital of Iraq is Baghdad.

The first **civilization** began in Iraq!

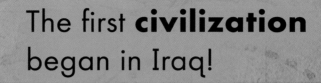

N
W — E
S

Baghdad,
Iraq

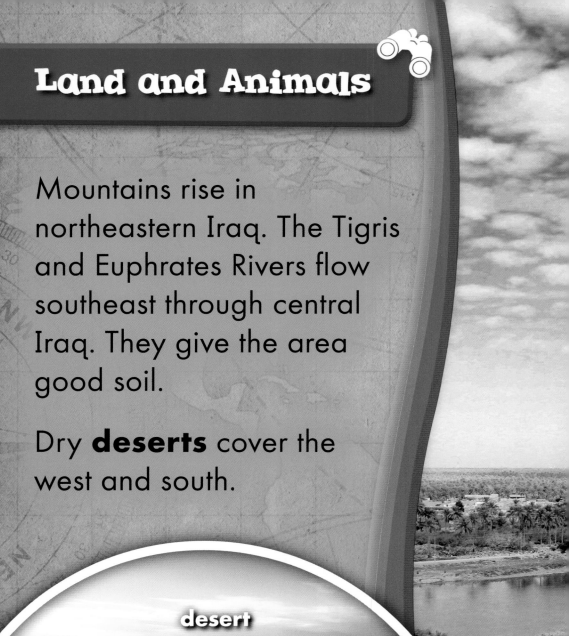

Land and Animals

Mountains rise in northeastern Iraq. The Tigris and Euphrates Rivers flow southeast through central Iraq. They give the area good soil.

Dry **deserts** cover the west and south.

desert

Euphrates River

Size: 1,740 miles (2,800 kilometers) long

Famous For:

- longest river in southwest Asia
- where civilization began

dust storm

Much of Iraq has hot summers and mild winters. Strong winds form dust storms year-round.

The mountains are cooler.
Snow is common each winter.

Partridges peck for seeds in the mountains. Hyenas run along rivers. Herons catch fish.

striped hyena

chukar partridge

grey heron

sand cat

Arabian horned viper

In the deserts, sand cats hunt at night. Vipers slide across the sand.

Most Iraqis are **Arabs**. They most often speak Arabic. **Kurds** make up a smaller group of Iraqis. They speak Kurdish.

Islam is practiced by almost all Iraqis.

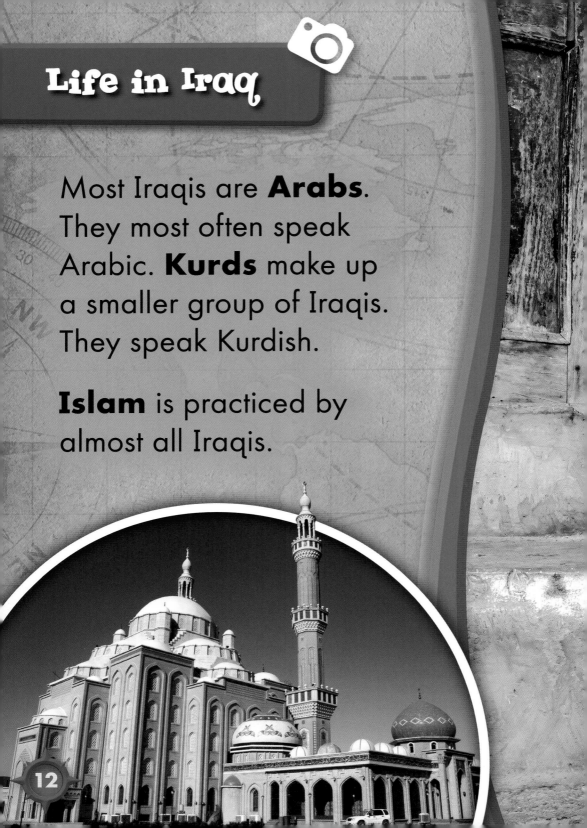

soccer

Soccer is a favorite sport.
People cheer for the national team.
Friends and family play together.

Men play board games in cafés. Women watch television at home.

board game

Masgouf is a fish dish enjoyed in Iraq. *Quzi* is lamb stuffed with rice and vegetables.

Iraqi Foods

masgouf

quzi

khubz

dates

Khubz is flatbread served
with many dishes.
Dates are eaten often.

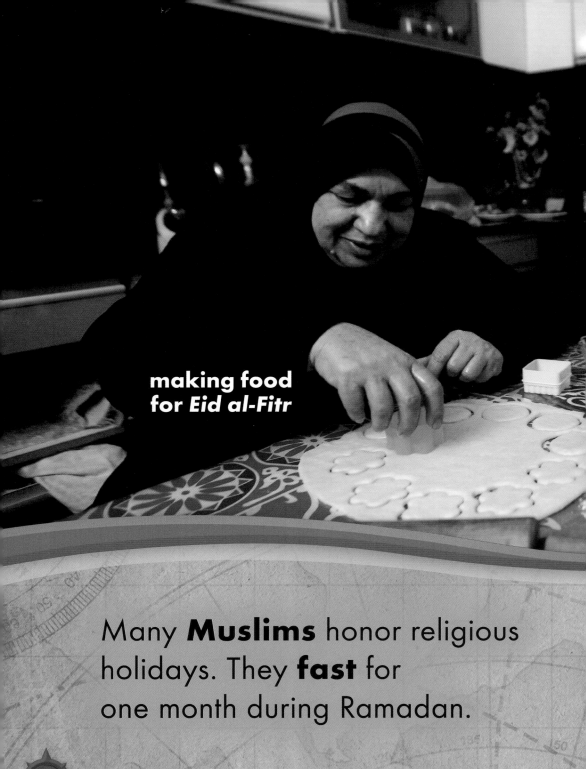

**making food
for *Eid al-Fitr***

Many **Muslims** honor religious
holidays. They **fast** for
one month during Ramadan.

Ramadan ends with *Eid al-Fitr*.
This holiday lasts for three days.
Families gather to eat and
give thanks!

Size:
169,235 square miles
(438,317 square kilometers)

Population:
40,462,701 (2022)

National Holidays:
Independence Day (October 3),
Republic Day (July 14)

Main Languages:
Arabic, Kurdish

Capital City:
Baghdad

Famous Face

Name: Nadia Murad

Famous For: in 2018, became
the first Iraqi to win a
Nobel Peace Prize

Religions

Christian: 1%

other: 4%

Muslim: 95%

Top Landmarks

Abbasid Palace

Ishtar Gate

Ziggurat of Ur

Glossary

Arabs—people who live mostly in the Middle East and northern Africa

civilization—a community with a set way of life

deserts—dry lands with few plants and little rainfall

fast—to stop eating all or some foods for a certain period of time

Islam—a religion based on belief in Allah as the only God and in Muhammad as God's follower

Kurds—people who mainly practice Islam and live in Turkey, Iran, Iraq, Syria, Armenia, and Azerbaijan

Middle East—a region of southwestern Asia and northern Africa; this region includes Egypt, Lebanon, Iran, Iraq, Israel, Saudi Arabia, Syria, and other nearby countries.

Muslims—people of the Islamic faith; Muslims follow the teachings of Muhammad as told to him from Allah.

To Learn More

AT THE LIBRARY

Leaf, Christina. *Zaha Hadid: Architect*. Minneapolis, Minn.: Bellwether Media, 2019.

Mattern, Joanne. *Iraq*. Minneapolis, Minn.: Pogo, 2019.

Zimmerman, Adeline J. *Ramadan*. Minneapolis, Minn.: Jump!, 2022.

ON THE WEB

FACTSURFER

Factsurfer.com gives you a safe, fun way to find more information.

1. Go to www.factsurfer.com.

2. Enter "Iraq" into the search box and click 🔍.

3. Select your book cover to see a list of related content.

Index